FISHERMAN
BIBLE STUDYGUIDES

ELIJAH

Obedience
in a Threatening World

ROBBIE CASTLEMAN

SHAW BOOKS

an imprint of WATERBROOK PRESS

Elijah

A SHAW BOOK

PUBLISHED BY WATERBROOK PRESS

2375 Telstar Drive, Suite 160

Colorado Springs, Colorado 80920

A division of Random House, Inc.

ISBN 0-87788-218-5

Printed in the United States of America

2005

10 9 8 7 6 5 4

Contents

How to Use This Studyguide

Fisherman studyguides are based on the inductive approach to Bible study. Inductive study is discovery study; we discover what the Bible says as we ask questions about its content and search for answers. This is quite different from the process in which a teacher *tells* a group *about* the Bible—what it means and what to do about it. In inductive study God speaks directly to each of us through his Word.

A group functions best when a leader keeps the discussion on target, but the leader is neither the teacher nor the "answer person." A leader's responsibility is to *ask*—not *tell*. The answers come from the text itself as group members examine, discuss, and think together about the passage.

There are four kinds of questions in each study. The first is an *approach question*. Asked and answered before the Bible passage is read, this question breaks the ice and helps you start thinking about the topic of the Bible study. It begins to reveal where thoughts and feelings need to be transformed by Scripture.

Some of the early questions in each study are *observation questions*—who, what, where, when, and how—designed to help you learn some basic facts about the passage of Scripture.

Once you know what the Bible says, you then need to ask, *What does it mean?* These *interpretation questions* help you to discover the writer's basic message.

Next come *application questions,* which ask, *What does it mean to me?* They challenge you to live out the Scripture's life-transforming message.

Fisherman studyguides provide spaces between questions for jotting down responses as well as any related questions you would like to raise in the group. Each group member should have a copy of the studyguide and may take a turn in leading the group.

A group should use any accurate, modern translation of the Bible such as the *New International Version,* the *New American Standard Bible,* the *New Revised Standard Version,* the *New Jerusalem Bible,* or the *Good News Bible.* (Other translations or paraphrases of the Bible may be referred to when additional help is needed.) Bible commentaries should not be brought to a Bible study because they tend to dampen discussion and keep people from thinking for themselves.

Suggestions for Group Leaders

1. Thoroughly read and study the Bible passage before the meeting. Get a firm grasp on its themes and begin applying its teachings for yourself. Pray that the Holy Spirit will "guide you into all truth" (John 16:13) so that your leadership will guide others.

2. If any of the studyguide's questions seem ambiguous or unnatural to you, rephrase them, feeling free to add others that seem necessary to bring out the meaning of a verse.

3. Begin (and end) the study promptly. Start by asking someone to pray that every participant will both understand the passage and be open to its transforming power. Remember, the Holy Spirit is the teacher, not you!

4. Ask for volunteers to read the passages aloud.

5. As you ask the studyguide's questions in sequence, encourage everyone to participate in the discussion. If some are silent, try gently suggesting, "Let's have an answer from someone who hasn't spoken up yet."

6. If a question comes up that you can't answer, don't be afraid to admit that you're baffled. Assign the topic as a research project for someone to report on next week, or say, "I'll do some studying and let you know what I find out."

7. Keep the discussion moving, but be sure it stays focused. Though a certain number of tangents are inevitable, you'll want to quickly bring the discussion back to the topic at hand. Also, learn to pace the discussion so that you finish the lesson in the time allotted.

8. Don't be afraid of silences; some questions take time to answer, and some people need time to gather courage to speak. If silence persists, rephrase your question, but resist the temptation to answer it yourself.

9. If someone comes up with an answer that is clearly illogical or unbiblical, ask for further clarification: "What verse suggests that to you?"

10. Discourage overuse of cross references. Learn all you can from the passage at hand, while selectively incorporating a few important references suggested in the studyguide.

11. Some questions are marked with a ⌀. This indicates that further information is available in the Leader's Notes at the back of the guide.

12. For further information on getting a new Bible study group started and keeping it functioning effectively, read *You Can Start a Bible Study Group* by Gladys Hunt and *Pilgrims in Progress: Growing Through Groups* by Jim and Carol Plueddemann. (Both books are available from Shaw Books.)

Suggestions for Group Members

1. Learn and apply the following ground rules for effective Bible study. (If new members join the group later, review these guidelines with the whole group.)

2. Remember that your goal is to learn all that you can *from the Bible passage being studied.* Let it speak for itself without using Bible commentaries or other Bible passages. There is more than enough in each assigned passage to keep your group productively occupied for one session. Sticking to the passage saves the group from insecurity ("I don't have the right reference books—or the time to read anything else.") and confusion ("Where did that come from? I thought we were studying _____.").

3. Avoid the temptation to bring up those fascinating tangents that don't really grow out of the passage you are discussing. If the topic is of common interest, you can bring it up later in informal conversation after the study. Meanwhile, help one another stick to the subject.

4. Encourage one another to participate. People remember best what they discover and verbalize for

themselves. Some people are naturally shy, while others may be afraid of making a mistake. If your discussion is free and friendly and you show real interest in what group members think and feel, the quieter ones will be more likely to speak up. Remember, the more people involved in a discussion, the richer it will be.

5. Guard yourself from answering too many questions or talking too much. Give others a chance to share their ideas. If you are one who participates easily, discipline yourself by counting to ten before you open your mouth.

6. Make personal, honest applications and commit yourself to letting God's Word change you.

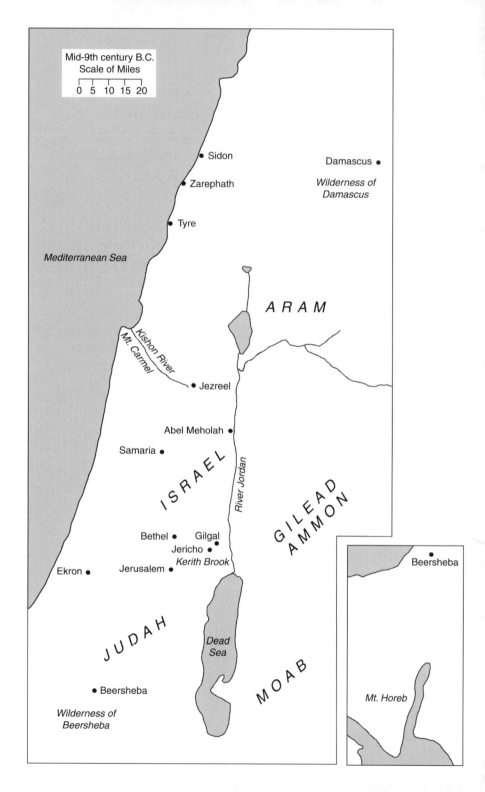

Obedience in a Threatening World

N eed help being obedient to God?
    Obedience is the mark of the wise person who survives the onslaught of a world that threatens to drown the people of God. Obedience means hearing the Word of God and *doing* what one hears.

> Therefore everyone who hears these words of mine and puts them into practice is like a wise man who built his house on the rock. The rain came down, the streams rose, and the winds blew and beat against that house; yet it did not fall, because it had its foundation on the rock. But everyone who hears these words of mine and does not put them into practice is like a foolish man who built his house on sand. The rain came down, the streams rose, and the winds blew and beat against that house, and it fell with a great crash. (Matthew 7:24-27)

Elijah was a master builder on the rock of faith. In the brief narrative of his life, Scripture records nine occasions when the mighty prophet heard the word of the Lord and, in spite of physical threats, spiritual droughts, emotional depression, and social abandonment, *did* what he *heard*. Elijah, by his example of obedience, has much to say to a world that congratulates the compromiser and shakes hands with sin for the sake of peace. In an age prone to when-it-feels-right obedience, he demonstrates a discipleship determined by will, not emotion. Yet his example can touch the callous modern heart with compelling tenderness.

I have always liked Elijah! He got things done. He took the bull by the horns and didn't bother to wait for a committee. Elijah confronted situations bluntly, and he zealously called the nation to shake itself free from sin. He was a man of action who saw the power of God working in his world, changing his people.

Elijah and I share some similarities—we both like the extraordinary, the dramatic, the swift revival. But we also share some weaknesses. So often in my years of discipleship I have experienced discouragement and depression when God did not act in my life with spectacular power. Indeed, it seemed at times that God was not present at all: nothing happened, no one changed. Elijah teaches me the potential perils of an obedience to God based only on results.

As you begin this study of Elijah, identify your own motives for being obedient to God. Set aside the pervasive attitude that makes results the reason for your obedience. Let Elijah show you that obedience carries with it no promise of power to change the situation. Obedience only promises the presence of God—and that will change *you!*

This Bible studyguide is designed to help you obey God in a threatening world. May you be challenged by the Word of God through a man who obeyed—Elijah the Tishbite.

Historical Review

It had been little more than fifty years since Israel had reached the zenith of its power during the reign of Solomon. In the meantime, the ten northern tribes—known as Israel—rebelled against the heavy burdens imposed by Solomon's son Rehoboam, king of Judah (1 Kings 12). Israel's king, Jeroboam, expanded the northern tribes' political rebellion against Judah by establishing two new centers of worship within Israel's borders. This kept his people from sacrificing to the Lord at the temple in Jerusalem, which remained under Judean control. When Jeroboam set up golden calves in these new worship centers, the nation swiftly slid into idolatry and degrading pagan practices (1 Kings 12:26-33).

The progressive decadence of Israel was a reflection of the willful disobedience of her kings. Nadab, the son of Jeroboam, ruled only two years and was murdered by Baasha. After a twenty-four-year reign that perpetuated the moral decline of the nation, Baasha was succeeded by his son Elah. After two years, Elah's servant Zimri conspired against his master, murdered Elah, and seized control of Israel. Zimri ruled only seven days! (1 Kings 14:20; 15:25-30; 15:33–16:15).

In a military coup supported by the people, Omri was declared king. Defeated, Zimri died in a fire lit by his own hand, and Omri reigned over Israel for twelve years. Upon his death, Omri's son Ahab began a twenty-two-year reign as the king of Israel (1 Kings 16:16-29).

Ahab, not content with the mere presence of idolatry, sought to establish Baal worship as the official religion of his realm. He married Jezebel, whose father was not only the king of Sidon, but, as a consequence of murdering his brother, was also the high priest of Baal worship. Jezebel would prove to be a true daughter of her ruthless father as she set out to destroy the worship of Yahweh, killing God's prophets with Ahab's mute consent (1 Kings 16:31-32; 18:13).

It was in these decadent, dark, and dangerous days that God sent his blazing firebrand to expose the sin of his people and to call the nation once more into the light of his mercy and love. To Israel's vilest king, God sent his greatest prophet: Elijah.

Obedience in Spite of the Times

1 KINGS 16:29–17:7

Wait 'til you see the whites of their eyes." This famous command given to the American soldiers at the Battle of Bunker Hill must have driven them to a point of desperation. Imagine watching the English troops coming closer—closer—*closer*—until it seemed they would certainly annihilate the American revolutionaries. Though these were men of action, they were not allowed to defend themselves until at last the command was given.

It wasn't that the revolutionaries weren't facing an urgent situation. The British were on the verge of hiring mercenaries to help put a stop to any demands for political and religious freedom in the colonies. War was breaking out in their homeland, and this battle proved it. Of course they wanted to attack as soon as possible. And yet they had to wait until their commander felt the time was appropriate.

Elijah, too, had to wait until his Commander let him know that the moment was right. After declaring that God would send a drought to the land of Israel because of its sin, he had to sit back and bide his time until the punishment took effect. And even after his own water source had dried up, when things were beginning to look desperate for him, he still obeyed this confusing order. It was not an easy thing for a man of action to do. In fact, it's seldom easy for any of us to obey God when we see trouble in the air and God's command is "Wait."

1. Describe a time in your life when you have known that God wanted you to wait. Discuss the results of your obedience or disobedience.

Right now. Bored with residency, Few friends who are not self consumed, feel waiting for something I was designed for.

Press On!

Saul, David, Solomon.
after Solomon civil war broke out → Israel in N, + Judah in South.

✎ **READ 1 KINGS 16:29–17:7.**

2. What characterized Ahab as a person and as a king? What effect did Ahab's rule have on the religious and domestic life of Israel (16:30-34)?

Evil + disobedient, did not obey God. Each king progressively more evil (v20 made by -Jeroboam) (v28+29 prevent people from goy to Jerusalem) Promoted idolatry. His wife essentially ruled. (we will discuss her + her implications later in this study)

---

3. No national protest was raised concerning the esca-
    lation of Baal worship in Israel. What does this indi-
    cate about Israel's attitude toward God at that time?
    Do you think the nation or Ahab intended to pro-
    voke the Lord by their idolatry?

They had become irreverant & wanted a god to fit their lifestyle more then a lifestyle to fit their God. No. they did it all out of convenience - travel, lesser load on their backs, less guilt perhaps.

4. Identify some situations in the world today that
    people (or nations) treat as trivial, but that could be
    provoking to God. What "small" concessions or
    "harmless" compromises did these situations begin
    with?

1) People find other ways to tithe.
2) Evolution only teaching in schools.

= Stem Cell
- Abortion

⚔ 5. *Elijah* means "whose God is Yahweh (Jehovah)."
What contrast do you see between Elijah's name,
whether given by his parents or assumed for his
ministry, and Ahab and his reign?

Elijah
"God is Yahweh"
Followed God
Come from nowhere?

Ahab

Followed everyone else's God
We have his whole history

⚔ 6. What was Elijah's abrupt proclamation to Ahab
(17:1)? What do Elijah's words tell you about his
relationship with God and his confidence in prayer?

Drought! He told the Baal worshiping king
whose god was supposed to bring rain, that
the Lord God of Israel would only bring
rain.

Complete confidence in His power + His
truth to Elijah.

Deut 11:16-17

7. What do you think Elijah learned from his experience by the brook Kerith? How would the Lord's
   provision of food have helped Elijah wait?

   Dependence. Ravens brought food + dependent on brook for water. He would know it was time to move on when brook dried up. yet he still waited.

8. Ravens are scavenger birds and were considered
   unclean according to Jewish law (Leviticus 11:13-
   15). How might this fact have influenced Elijah's
   faith at that time? What might he have felt when
   the brook dried up?

9. What did Elijah need to hear before he left the
   brook—even though it dried up? Which do you
   think was easier for Elijah—confronting Ahab
   publicly or waiting by the brook privately?

   Time to go (17v9)

   Confronting Ahab. He didn't know how long to wait by the brook. You can muster up courage, but not time / patience.

10. Is it easier for you to *do* the will of God or *wait* in the will of God? What is difficult about each?

Do. Waiting is so hard. Perhaps why I'm waiting now.

11. *Kerith* means "the cutting place." Explain how waiting in a difficult situation can be a "cutting place" in your life.

Refuel vs.

✐ 12. Identify some modern-day Ahabs. How might you confront these people with the judgment of the living God?

✐ 13. Summarize how Elijah's example can help you obey God in spite of the threatening times we live in.

Obedience in Spite of Circumstances

1 KINGS 17:7-24

The student from Zimbabwe finishes his sermon, and the offertory hymn begins, "Bringing in the sheaves, bringing in the sheaves, We shall come rejoicing, bringing in the sheaves!" Suddenly, you hear that familiar voice, "Contribute. You've learned today of the lives that are being touched in Africa, and I want you to participate."

"But, God," you contest, "I've barely got enough money to get by this month! I had to have all that work done on my car, and my Visa bill is already much higher than I'll be able to pay off, and the plumbing needs fixing, and you never know what *other* crisis may come up…" Still, you hear: "Give." And you wonder why God so frequently tells you to do such hard things when you're already in desperate circumstances.

As the drought continued, Elijah's face was pasted on every "Wanted" poster in King Ahab's realm. On top of that, his hiding place, the brook Kerith, had become a dry creek bed. Still Elijah prayed and followed God's direction instead of determining God's will on the basis of his desperate circumstances. This was a lesson the prophet's next provider needed to learn, too.

1. Describe a time when you have obeyed God despite difficult circumstances. How did he provide for you in that situation?

Now. Always by me— will always listen, even when I am irrational + demanding.

READ 1 KINGS 17:7-16.

2. Why did Elijah leave Kerith (verses 7-10)? Why was Zarephath (a city in Sidon) a dangerous place for him to go? (Hint: Who was king of Sidon at that time? See 1 Kings 16:31.) How might the wait at Kerith have strengthened Elijah's obedience?

— God told him to go to Zarepheth.
— Sidon was full of Baal worshipers.
— The waiting time made him completely trust God.

Kerith means to cut off or to cut down

↳ Needed to be cut down + cut off to rely totally on God.

3. Who did Elijah encounter at the gate of Zarephath? Why did this widow seem an unlikely person to have received the Lord's command to provide for Elijah?

A widow (a gentile). - Jesus speaks on this in Luke 4:25-26. - God sometimes chooses Gentiles for His work.

- We continue to see Elijah stretched - 1st ravens which are unclean for provision - 2nd a Gentile woman for provision.

4. Compare the widow's responses to Elijah's request for water from the *public* well and his request for bread from her *private* resources.

No rebuttal appears to have been made concerning water - but regarding food (she thought she was preparing her last meal).

5. What did the widow recognize about Elijah (verse 12)? What effect might this realization have had on her obedience to the Lord's command to feed the prophet?

That he was a man of the living God. She felt a loneliness + need for Him.

Application:

6. The drought threatened this widow and her son
   with starvation. How might this situation have
   affected her attitude toward Elijah? How might it
   have influenced her decision to obey God?

*She may have seen it
as a burden yet she recognized
God in Elijah + obeyed him.*

*made it more (?)
difficult to learn
trust under these
circumstances.*

7. Discuss specific prejudices and preconceptions that
   influence your response to God's will. In what ways
   does God "speak" to you today? How do you
   respond to his words?

Small urgings. - Uncomfortability.

*Often in defiance only reluctantly
giving in when realizing no
other choice.*

8. In what ways can material possessions be an obstacle to personal obedience? Share times when your obedience to God's will was affected by either your slim or your abundant resources.

- We can learn to rely on them only.
- Difficult to tithe when bills come in, but sure feel obediant (prideful). Pretty easy to obey in times of plenty.

READ 1 KINGS 17:17-24.

9. How might Elijah's promise in 1 Kings 17:14 have heightened the grief the widow felt over the death of her son? What did she identify as the reason for her son's death? How did she express her anger (verse 18)?

The drought may have been contributing factor to his death - yet she blamed Elijah for "ordering" his death for some iniquity she may have committed.
"What do I have to do?"

10. Compare the way Elijah handled his confusion and feelings with the way the widow dealt with hers. Which response is most like yours?

- She lashed out + asked what she had to do - other than trust him. (blame others)
- Elijah had a plan + went to God 1st for a solution.

11. It was against Jewish law for a priest or prophet to touch a corpse (Leviticus 22:4). Discuss Elijah's prayer and action in the light of this prohibition.

Calamity? Elijah was learning about God's use of others — ravens, widow for his care. He may have understood saving God even if it conflicted with Jewish law. He may have a glimpse @ Jesus.

12. According to the widow's words in verse 24, what had she learned from the experience of having her son returned to her alive? Specifically, how would this display of God's power diminish the power of circumstances to determine her obedience to God's will?

She now had her thoughts confirmed regarding Elijah.
She had been brought through draught, sure starvation, + her son's death unscathed. she was learning trust.

13. In what ways can your obedience to God's Word be influenced by circumstances in your life? (Consider the influence of both positive and negative factors.) How does Elijah's life challenge your thinking about knowing and doing God's will?

Time in God's word certainly Δ's $\bar{c}$ the months.

Much more obedient @ the extremes - to change bad circumstances or to continue good. Harder in middle of the road.

Elijah always obeyed - no matter how ludicrous, how absurd, or if God used unusual ways to provide for Elijah.

Obedience in Spite of Danger

1 KINGS 18:1-18

C ourage. What an alarming word. *The American Heritage Dictionary* defines it as "the state or quality of mind or spirit that enables one to face danger with self-possession, confidence, and resolution." *Courage* means doing things that don't make sense—overstepping reason and ignoring the possible consequences. And for what? Because something is so important that we know we must do it.

Elijah was no coward. After living with the widow in Zarephath of Sidon for approximately two years, he followed the Lord's command to return home and confront the evil Ahab. It was an insane risk, for as the drought had turned Israel's soil to fruitless dust, a furious Ahab had intensified his search for the prophet who had caused such misery. And yet Elijah resolutely pressed on toward a confrontation with the king. He may have been wary of what God was leading him into, but his spirit was confident. He would obey this command, for his courage came from the Lord.

1. Describe a time when God gave you, someone you
    know, or someone you've read about courage to face
    a dangerous predicament.

READ 1 KINGS 18:1-18.

2. Why did Elijah return to Israel? What influence
    might the condition of the drought-stricken land
    have had on his response to God's command to go
    meet Ahab?

    - God had shown him it was the *
      time for the drought to end as well.

    - Everyone was looking for Elijah, almost
      as if they thought Elijah was responsible,
      yet he was just the messenger
      (made it much more difficult).

3. Elijah's prompt obedience is all the more amazing in
    the face of Jezebel's attack on the Lord's prophets
    (verse 4) and Ahab's frantic search for him (verse
    10). In light of his example, discuss your level of
    obedience when physical harm or hardship is a real

possibility. How do the lives of Elijah and other biblical figures challenge the current teaching about "successful" discipleship? What is successful discipleship according to this passage?

So easy to just be quiet.

- *Successful discipleship comes from taking a stand - often against "powerful" people & obeying God.*

- *Telling people truth, even if not what they want to hear.*

4. Whom did Obadiah identify as his master? Whom did Elijah identify as Obadiah's master (verse 8)? What conflict and compromise in Obadiah's allegiance became apparent in this interaction?

He identified Elijah, yet Elijah saw Obadiah's heart & identified Ahab as his master.
- How did Elijah know this?

5. What reasons did Obadiah give for his strong reluctance to obey Elijah's command? Why did Obadiah tell Elijah that he had hidden the prophets?

- Thought he had sinned or wanted it pointed out. Obadiah wanted acknowledgment for his works of hiding prophets.

- Justification by works, thought he would meet certain death for what he was being asked to do.

6. What was Elijah's response to Obadiah's lengthy protest? What did Elijah know *for sure* that bolstered his uncompromising obedience?

Similar to Daniel 3

- Elijah will reveal himself to Ahab.
- Our God is the Living God, & God would soon reveal this on Mt Carmel.

7. How can an unwavering trust in God, in spite of danger, help you obey him? What other factors might help you be obedient in difficult and dangerous situations?

- There is no danger if we have true trust in omnipotent God.

- Past experience of God's protection & provision which Elijah had at Cherith as well.

8. What did Ahab say to Elijah when they met? What did his description of Elijah reflect about his feeling toward his own sin and the sin of his country?

- ... "You troubler of Israel."
  What kind of insight does Ahab have?

- He did not take responsibility for or didn't know he was responsible for the drought & decline.

9. What two reasons did Elijah give for Israel's current dilemma (verse 18)? How are these reasons related to each other?

> - His actions & his fathers' actions
> - Sins are passed down from generation.
>   - what does this mean??
>   _____
>   Teaching sinful patterns to those

10. In what ways are the nations of the world today in the same kind of trouble that Ahab and the nation of Israel were in? What are some of the consequences of turning away from God?

> - We are on a slow moral decline, & we don't repent or turn aside from our sinful ways.
>
> - Turn away from God, you may get what /will get what you're asking for.

11. Describe Elijah's attitude as he confronted King Ahab. What was the source of his security?

> Confidence in the Creator.   Trust in God
>
> - Experience?
> - How do we go through that 1st exper?

12. Identify personal attitudes, actions, or compromises that currently trouble your own "kingdom" (your home, your workplace, your church, etc.). What rebuke, caution, or command does God's Word bring to you? How can Elijah's example encourage you to obey the Lord's will in spite of physical strain, hardship, or danger?

    Trust in all.

Obedience in Spite of Impossibilities

1 KINGS 18:19-40

G od, I pray, light these idle sticks of my life and may I burn for you. Consume my life, my God, for it is yours. I seek not a long life, but a full one, like you, Lord Jesus."

This prayer of missionary Jim Elliot was fulfilled when the Auca Indians, to whom he was ministering, killed him and four other missionaries. His sacrificial spirit was remarkable. But the faith of his wife Elisabeth was perhaps even more amazing.

After her husband's brutal death, Elisabeth picked up herself and her young daughter and marched right back to the South American Indians to bring them to God. Those of us who hear her story are left stunned. How could she be sure these threatening pagan enemies wouldn't kill her, too? Yet the love she extended and the courage she demonstrated brought rich rewards—the Aucas saw Christ in her and wanted to hear more about the one who enabled this woman to take on such an impossible challenge.

Elijah was in just that situation. The time had come for

him to march into his enemies' camp and bring them to God. And how was he to do this? By setting up an offering on an altar, drenching it in the priceless water of the land, and expecting fire to come from the sky and burn it up. How utterly impossible! When the pagan prophets spent the entire day failing to make the impossible happen, Elijah might understandably have preferred to forget the whole thing. But he didn't—he obeyed God's instruction once again. And because of his obedience and faith, God brought about an impossible victory.

1.   Describe an impossible situation you have faced or are facing in your life.

READ 1 KINGS 18:19-29.

2.   Who assembled for the Mount Carmel contest? Briefly suggest reasons for the people's journey to Carmel.

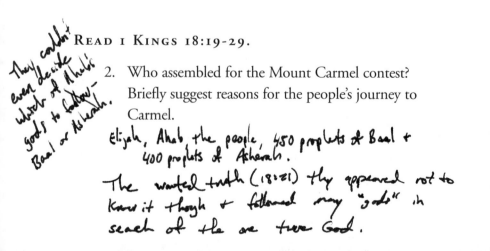

They couldn't even decide which of Ahab's gods to follow. Baal or Asherah.

Elijah, Ahab, the people, 450 prophets of Baal + 400 prophets of Asherah.

The wanted truth (18:21) they appeared not to know it though + followed many "gods" in search of the one true God.

3. How did Elijah summarize the nation's spiritual dilemma in his first confrontation with the people? Why did the people have no answer for him?

They were lukewarm - this is certainly addressed in Revelation as well.

1) Elijah was correct
2) They knew truth, but enjoyed the sin following Ahab's religion allowed
3) Some weren't sure

4. Considering the circumstances of the previous three and a half years, what do you think the people thought of Elijah? Why?

Some may have hated him + felt he was responsible for the drought, some may have feared him for the power they thought he possessed, some may have looked up to his courage against an ungodly king.

5. Summarize the contest rules and how the winner was to be determined. What did the people's response to the <u>proposal indicate about</u> their attitudes?   *1 Kings 18:24b*

They would each offer a sacrifice + then call on their god to light it. the lit sacrifice would be the one true god.

They were willing to believe anything, they had no preconceived notions, hopes, or attitudes as to who would win. They were spiritually clueless.

✓ 6.   Read verse 21 again. Under what circumstances
       does an attitude of ⟦wavering⟧ tend to creep into
       your life? How does this vacillating inhibit your
       own spiritual growth? the growth of the church?

*Consistency with God. Hard to have a
deep relationship when only one of you is
speaking + the other doesn't listen or
doesn't answer (me). This makes it
hard to lead in the Church.*

7.   Describe the efforts of the prophets of Baal to get
     their god to answer their prayers. How does the bib-
     lical account emphasize the futility of their efforts?

The wailed all about

8.   Identify false gods in today's world that make great
     demands of us but give us no answers. In what ways
     should your recognition of these "gods" influence
     the priorities you set?

*Fame.
Fortune.
Power.
Knowledge.*

Read 1 Kings 18:30-40.

9. How did repairing the altar help the people to
   understand their sin? Considering the extent of the
   drought, what did Elijah's command to pour their
   scarce water over the offering require of the people?

It had previously been destroyed.

*Some degree of faith, but certainly effort
if they had to walk to sea to obtain it.*

10. Why is an attitude of dependence on God necessary
    when we pray? What do you have to "pour out"
    before you can more fully rely on God to answer
    prayer?

11. Why did Elijah address the Lord in his prayer the
    way he did? What specific petitions did he make?
    What reason did he give for his prayer to be
    answered?

12. Describe how the people reacted after God's miraculous answer to Elijah's prayer. How would slaughtering the Baal prophets help restore the people's faith and obedience? _- was this necessary?_

13. Elijah's experience shows us that obedience and idolatry cannot mix. For personal revival (rain!) to come, we must forsake disobedience and ask God to forgive us. What needs to happen to put an end to ("slaughter") any idol worship in your life? What can we do to identify and purge the idolatry in the life of the corporate church?

Obedience in Spite of Delay

1 Kings 18:41-46

The country of Austria is known as a graveyard of missions. But Jeff and Anita Bradley felt God calling them there, packed up their little household, and went. They found the Austrians outwardly pleasant, but inwardly distant. The young couple tried for five years, but no one was interested in getting to know them—or God. Ten years later, they had a small group coming to their home once a week, but none of the folks seemed interested in committing their lives to Christ.

A few weeks after their twenty-year anniversary on the mission field, the Bradleys discussed going home, not for a furlough, but for good. It seemed that God wasn't planning to use them for his kingdom after all. But the voice of God was still strong in their hearts, and they knew that to leave would mean disobeying that voice.

At last, one spiritually searching young man came to their small group. They introduced him to Jesus and dedicated themselves to discipling this one convert. In three months, he had brought six of his university friends to the group, and four of them had also accepted Christ. Soon, Jeff and Anita were going to the campus every week to conduct Bible studies for other seekers. No midlife crisis for this couple—they were reaping a harvest of souls!

When God told Elijah it would not rain until Elijah spoke the word, the prophet may have been able to see that drought was certain. But three years later, when God told him to let Ahab know it would rain again, the blue skies and blazing sun must have made Elijah doubt. And when he was forced to send his servant again and again to search for a cloud—*any* cloud— that might assure that what he'd said was true, he had a great opportunity to quit and go home. Fortunately for the people of Israel, Elijah didn't stop believing. He obeyed the voice he had learned to trust. And at last, the rain poured from heaven.

1. How do you react when God takes a long time to answer your prayers?

   Impatiently + wonder if ever. Maybe my prayer at that time was never going to be answered as it's outside His will.
   Other times God answers quickly.

READ I KINGS 18:41-46.

2. What did Elijah say to Ahab to indicate that he expected rain (verse 41)? What do Elijah's words reveal about his faith that God would bring rain despite the lack of evidence in the skies?

   ....the sound of a heavy shower.
   Elijah had learned to trust God. His time in Cherith, in Zarephath + now on the mountain in front of the worshipers of Baal + Asherah + Ahab when he was protected + used by God.

3. Where did Elijah go during the feast? Why?

To the top of Mt. Carmel.

To pray that God's will would be done — he may have expected instant downpour of rain which didn't occur.

4. What did the prophet's body posture indicate about his attitude toward God? Why did he pray for something God had already promised?

Elijah understood penitence + God's holiness. It is an act of obedience + submission to be on our knees.

Elijah didn't know God's timing.

God's response: continue to perfect us.

5. How do you think Elijah's servant felt as he reported six times, "There is nothing there"? What might his wording of the seventh report indicate about his faith?

He either understood that God could easily work through such a small cloud, or he was giving up mentioning a cloud as small as a man's hand.

6. What was Elijah's response to the seventh report? Why did he instruct Ahab and the people to go down the mountain before the heavy rain?

Elijah knew it was time + he definitely knew what God could do with very little.

(the widow + her flour)

7. Elijah was able to arrive in Jezreel (about twenty miles away) before Ahab. What enabled Elijah to accomplish this amazing feat (verse 46)? Why might he have needed to get there first?

God enabled him to arrive first to ensure the story was told correctly.

8. Pause and think seriously about your prayer life, identifying specific strengths and weaknesses. What is the most difficult aspect of praying for you?

Praying for long periods of time.

Being faithful to pray for things even when prayer is not answered.

Great faith takes great commitment.

9. What encouragement do you find in praying? Are you usually encouraged by results after you pray or by something else while you are praying? Explain your answer.

Communion c̄ God. Encouraged by God's comfort + God's reassurance.

God's answers don't always come in our time nor do they have to. God is omnipotent + knows when answers must come before it's too late, not when we think it's to late.

10. Share examples of persistent, obedient prayer from your own experience, from Scripture, or from the experience of someone you know or have read about.

11. Identify and share one specific need for God's healing "rain" in your life. If you are in a group, give everyone in the group an opportunity to share one need. Then pray specifically for each need.

Forgiveness. I struggle c̄ true forgiveness to those I feel "wronged" by.

*Spend time in prayer on our knees/floor together. *

Obedience in Spite of Discouragement

1 KINGS 19:1-18

The words of the old American folk song "Home on the Range" express so well our longing for a life without discouragement:

> *Oh, give me a home where the buffalo roam*
> *where the deer and the antelope play!*
> *Where seldom is heard a discouraging word*
> *and the skies are not cloudy all day.*

We all might not care to live near a herd of buffalo, but we certainly wouldn't mind never being discouraged. In fact, we usually try to run from discouragement, taking extra care to keep ourselves from having any expectations so that we won't be disappointed when they aren't fulfilled. But when the old letdowns resurface—and they always will—our whole world comes crashing down.

After God had given victory to Elijah on Mount Carmel and the rain had come in answer to Elijah's prayers, Queen Jezebel made a frenzied threat to kill God's prophet. No one came running to help or to shelter him; in fact, Elijah didn't seem to have a friend on earth. His world came to a screeching halt: This was not what he'd expected.

In his discouragement, Elijah stumbled in his obedient walk with the Lord. His fear-driven disobedience can help us anticipate our own tendency to run and hide when the going gets tough. But in the foreground, as we peek into Elijah's depression, we see God, who in his mercy proved to be as patient with his disobedient prophet as he'd always been—and always is with his disobedient people.

1. On a scale of one to ten, how discouraged do you typically feel when things don't go your way? In what ways does discouragement show up in your everyday life?

READ 1 KINGS 19:1-9.

2. Having just experienced the extraordinary power of God on Mount Carmel and the successful campaign of prayer for rain, what do you think Elijah anticipated as he sped towards Jezreel, the headquarters of Jezebel and the nation's center of Baal worship?

Relief + the arrival of God's Kingdom?

A changed land?

⚔ 3. What was Elijah's reaction to Jezebel's threat? What important detail was missing in Elijah's sudden deci-sion to begin this journey?

Fear. He did not pray or seek God until it was purely reactionary.

Beersheba
Gen 21:31   — why Beer^{sh}? 25 — 17:11

⚔ 4. What factors might have contributed to Elijah's reaction? How did his desire in verse 4 contradict the very reason he ran away?

Fatigue. He ran to preserve his life, then asked to die stating he 'had had enough.'

Read

Numbers 11:10-15

⚔ 5. Briefly summarize God's treatment of his fearful and fatigued prophet. What did God do? What did he not do?

God provided him c̄ comfort + strength to carry on.
God knows what we can + cannot bear.

6. Share situations in your experience when physical fatigue contributed to your inaccurate perception of the circumstances. What practical steps can you take to avoid wrong decisions influenced by physical—or emotional—weariness?

Prayer & seek counsel from those stronger and/or wiser than us.

7. What did God ask Elijah when he reached Mount Horeb? What did God's question indicate about his opinion of the prophet's "retirement"?

What are you doing here?
It wasn't the yet for his retirement, God had/has additional plan for Elijah.

READ 1 KINGS 19:10-18.

8. What attitudes did Elijah's response convey? Discuss some other ways people attempt to justify their disobedience.

He tells God all the things he has done for Him.

We tend to weigh our good & bad deeds.

9. What was God teaching Elijah by refusing to show himself in the exciting displays of nature's power? What did God say to Elijah after the gentle whisper?

God doesn't always reveal himself in grand displays; often / sometimes just a quiet ~~whisper~~ whisper.

— Told Elijah the next step in his ministry.

10. Why did God ask Elijah the same question again? If you were doing a dramatic reading of this passage, would Elijah's two replies to God sound the same or different? Why?

He asked him again to see if Elijah would admit to his fault.
Elijah may have been almost broken repeating his answer again.

11. Summarize God's remedy for Elijah's depression and self-righteous retirement. What effect might Elisha's appointment as God's prophet and the news of the seven thousand faithful people have had on him?

these occur when we are self focused

Elijah thought he was alone. He was probably very encouraged to hear others had remained faithful + that another would take his place.

12. Discuss how the exciting mountaintop experiences of faith affect your daily life. Are you prone, like Elijah, to want God to continue spectacular works of grace in the valleys of your life? If so, where do you run when God does not eliminate all the Jezebels of opposition that you face?

I went to continue the feeling of being filled by God during spiritual peaks. - it's so easy to give up in valleys + focus on ourselves.

13. In what ways might sullenness and disobedience be indications of pride? How can teamwork or accountability with others counter this tendency toward pride in your life or in the life of your church?

We can do it.

Learn to rely on those around us.

Obedience in Spite of Martyrdom

1 KINGS 21

It's been said that only the good die young, but one English author and humorist insisted: "Only the young die good." It seems the more time we spend living "the good life," the more time we have to be bad! And then when we *do* try to live righteously, someone or something is always getting in the way. For Naboth, that someone was the king of Israel, and the something was treacherous murder. Naboth obeyed God's command, but because of his obedience, he made a powerful enemy. The result? Another good man met an early death.

But there's more to the story. What happens to those who aren't good—those who have racked up enough evils to sentence them for life? After causing so much trouble in both his nation and his neighborhood, King Ahab had earned a death sentence, and Elijah was called to deliver it. While this study focuses on Naboth's obedience, we see Elijah, too, obeying in the face of his own potential martyrdom.

◊ 1.   What examples have you seen of martyrdom? Why do you suppose this so often happens to the righteous?

Columbine HS

◊ **READ 1 KINGS 21.**

◊ 2.   What reason did Naboth give for refusing Ahab's request? Describe the king's reaction to Naboth's decision, including what he did and didn't do.

"The Lord forbid me that I should give you the inheritance of my fathers."
— Ahab pouted + spoke to the real head of the household — his wife.
— He did accept NO. (s) (Num 36:7)
Why did Naboth refuse

3.   Summarize Jezebel's attitude towards Ahab, Naboth, and God's Law.

Jezebel treated him as a child (Ahab) Naboth as insignificant, + God's law as beneath her wishes.

4. What did the necessary acquisition of false witnesses reflect about Naboth's character? How did his refusal to sell his land to Ahab reflect his character and the value he placed on obedience to God's word?

Naboth's character was not in question & no one could be found to honestly accuse him.

He placed God, & rightly so, above all others.

5. What price did Naboth pay for being obedient to God? In what ways can living in obedience to the Lord cause problems for you in the world?

Matt 10:39 He who has find.

Martyrdom. Certainly not PC, as Christianity despite its grace is often described as intolerant. Also hard to stand apart & being accused of intolerance.

6. What was Ahab's reaction to the treachery of Jezebel? What impression of Ahab do you get from this scene in his life?

He was fine with it, accepted what he was wrongfully given.

Poor - No leadership.

7. What was God's attitude concerning the death of
Naboth? Prior to Elijah's arrival, what was Ahab's
attitude toward Naboth's death? What was he doing?

Ahab's final straw— he was enjoying
his new "inheritance."

8. What did Ahab's greeting to Elijah reveal about the
state of his conscience (verse 20)? According to
Elijah, what was Ahab's sin?

He knew. Sold himself, his
righteousness if any existed, for
land.
Yet still didn't admit his sin,
called Elijah his enemy for
his convicting influence.
- Do we know people like this?

9. In what ways can we show our obedience to God by
the quantity and cost of our worldly possessions and
by our attitudes toward them?

Willing to let ... go.

Lev 25:23

10. Jezebel thought she obtained Naboth's vineyard for
nothing. What, in fact, did it cost her? How and
why was her punishment worse than Ahab's?

Her life.

How did both die? 1 Ky 22:34-38
Ahab - shot by chance + died in his chariot
ē dogs licking up his blood.
Jezebel - 2 Kings 9:33 killed by Jehu who
was anointed by Elijah (1 Kn 19:15-17) +
(Elisha 2 Kn 9:6) + 2 Ky 9
25-26

11. Even though he was not the instigator of Naboth's
murder, why did God declare Ahab guilty? What
important caution does this incident give us concerning the oppression of the poor in our day?

- He was head of the household, + accepted
what he knew he was wrongfully given.

- Help those in need, don't take advantage
of our place or theirs.

12. What was Ahab's reaction to Elijah's word of judgment? ① What indications were there that Ahab's
repentance was sincere? ②

① Knew it was true + repented +
humbled himself before God.
Ahab had had front row tickets to
all of God's work through Elijah, he
had listened to others too long.

- God reduced his punishment

13. What "word of the Lord" would you probably have
      preferred to hear and deliver to the evil king if you
      had been in Elijah's place? Why? How does this
      incident increase your understanding of God's
      mercy?

Andy
Missi + work
DJ

Obedience in Spite of Offense

2 KINGS 1

Scottish poet Robert Burns once wrote some stanzas of advice to a young friend who was just launching into his adult life. In the poem he remarks: "An atheist-laugh's a poor exchange for Deity offended." Considering Burns's situation at that time—his true love had rejected him, taking with her all his hopes of marriage—he may very well have written those words of counsel with some firsthand regrets in mind!

Ahab's son Ahaziah could have profited from the advice of this eighteenth-century poet. Following in the footsteps of his mother Jezebel, King Ahaziah continued the spread of idolatry throughout the weakening nation of Israel. And so, although it lasted only two years, his reign was remarkably offensive to God.

The story opens with the king insulting God, and it quickly moves into a derisive attack on God's prophet. Elijah could have grumbled and turned his nose up at the taunting of Ahaziah's squadrons. But he had a better answer for every offense: the wrath of God. He might understandably have been wary of meeting the one who had sent those men to offend him, but he still obeyed God's directions and delivered the message of judgment to Ahaziah. The king would live only long enough to realize that his jeering laughter was a sad substitute for the happiness he could never claim.

1. Tell about a time when you were the target of a direct attack because you follow God's ways. How did you feel and what did you do about it?

READ 2 KINGS 1.

2. What was the cause of Ahaziah's illness? Why did he send messengers to Baal-Zebub?

Fell through the lattice To see if he would live.

3. Why did Elijah intercept Ahaziah's messengers? What did he ask them? How did God judge Ahaziah for his unbelief and disobedience?

God told him to.

with death.

4. From the messengers' description, how did Ahaziah know that the man who spoke to them was Elijah (verses 7-8)?

From his description

5. What action did King Ahaziah take to deal with his enemy? What did this response reveal about his attitude toward the Lord? Why would this action be offensive to both God and Elijah?

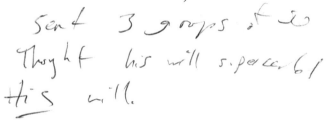

Sent 3 groups of mw
Thought his will s.pece 6/
his will.

6. Share some experiences in your life when you have "gone to Ekron"—anywhere away from God—for answers only he could supply. Consider specific circumstances in your life that tend to paralyze your obedience to God. Why is obedience difficult during those times?

Chase our own desires

7. Compare carefully the words and attitudes of each captain of fifty. Compare Elijah's response to each captain and the resulting action of God.

Called down judgment on them

8. What had the third captain learned that affected his attitude toward Elijah (verses 13-14)? Describe how your knowledge of God's judgment influences your faith and obedience?

Humility. He knew he was no match for God's awesome power.

✗ 9. What indicates that Elijah might have been afraid to go to Ahaziah? Why do you think this was the case? What kind of risk did Elijah take by following God's command?

Jezebel was his mom 2 King 9:33

10. Why is God's judgment on sin often difficult to present to people today? (See Romans 6:23.) Think of as many reasons as you can.

Judgement –

Free will has been taken over by free rights

11. What can you learn from Elijah that encourages you to speak the whole truth to "dying" people so that they have a chance to repent—even if they've offended you?

Elijah was protected
It is easy to cut off them – but God didnt do that too. /

Obedience in Spite of Death

2 KINGS 2:1-14

You've undoubtedly heard it a hundred times: Nothing is certain but death and taxes. Taxes are bad enough, but death is even harder to handle. It's a journey into the unknown, a critical test in trusting God.

During the ten years that followed Elisha's call, Elijah was occupied with his "quiet" work. The two men of God, in defiance of Jezebel, reestablished schools for the training and teaching of other prophets who would proclaim God's word. These primitive seminaries helped sustain a faithful remnant of Israelites who would not kneel to Baal. During Elijah's final days he visited these schools one last time.

As he did, the certainty of death hung heavily over him. The *un*certainty about exactly what would happen could easily have kept him from trusting—and obeying—God. But Elijah faithfully obeyed to the end, and God rewarded him.

1. When you think of dying, what are you afraid of?
   Why might it be harder—or easier—to obey God
   when you're preparing to die?

   Suffering & pain.

   *You know its temporary & will see
   Him soon.*

READ 2 KINGS 2:1-14.

2. What places did Elijah and Elisha visit prior to
   crossing the Jordan? How might these visits have
   encouraged Elijah?

   1 Kings 18:11 - Obadiah Bethel, Jericho, Jordan.
   1 Kings 19:14 ... I alone am left.
   *Now he sees others that can carry
   out God's work → Elishah & their students.*
   Have to be able to pass on your faith!

3. How did Elisha show his love and support for Elijah
   during this last journey? What did the prophets-in-
   training do to show their concern and respect for
   Elijah before he was taken away?

   He would not leave him.

   *- They came out to see them &
   told Elisha what he knew already, be silent
   he was being prepared for ministry too sad.
   alone - as a mature prophet.*
   *Told literally "he will be removed from his head"
   as a student sits below his master*

4. Elijah's final teachings must have contained important advice and exhortation for the student prophets. If you knew you had only a short time to live, what vital information would you share, and with whom? How would your daily activities reflect these priorities?

Little is important in this life other than people + God.

~~Work~~

~~money~~ ~~computers~~ ~~sports~~

So little matters.
I would work only enough for sustenance.

5. Elijah wanted to die east of the Jordan in his homeland of Gilead. What did he do to show his concern for Elisha, his faithful companion and coworker? What did Elisha request in verses 9 and 10? Why do you think he made this request?

Gave him a request - Elijah brought up the question - not Elisha

A double portion of Elijah's spirit be upon Elisha. ⌐ Deut 21:17 ⌐ right of the firstborn
Gen 25:31 (inheritance)

only to be Elijah's worthy successor.

— birthright was a double portion + would be the family's leader.

Elijah ~~pulled~~ 8 recorded miracles + Elisha 16.

6. Why did Elijah feel *he* could not grant Elisha's request? How did he leave the decision in God's hand? Besides the condition of this blessing, why would it have been important to Elisha to see Elijah depart?

> — Knew it was up to God.
> — By what events would unfold.
> — To know where he had gone.

7. What were the two prophets doing when Elijah was taken from the earth? Looking carefully at the passage, describe how Elijah was taken to heaven.

> Walking & talking ē each other.
> Horses of fire separated them from one another & Elijah was taken.

8. What words did Elisha cry out as Elijah was taken up? What significance did this have for Elisha's ministry in the future?

> My father, my father, the chariots of Israel & its horsemen!
> Elijah saw it, yet others could not/did not showing the blessing upon Elijah.

9. How would Elijah's incredible departure influence Elisha's obedience in fulfilling the ministry given to him? How did Elisha demonstrate the power of his inheritance?

No doubts.

Immediately on waters c̄ cloak just as Elijah had done.

— ensure that God was with him

10. Read 2 Timothy 4:5-8, a portion of Paul's final letter to his student and coworker Timothy. Though we don't know the content of Elijah's final exhortation to Elisha as "they were walking along and talking" (2 Kings 2:11), perhaps it was similar to Paul's final words. How did Paul describe his life of obedience? How does joyful expectancy (our longing "for [Christ's] appearing") grow out of a life of daily, faithful obedience?

Not easy!

endomg, work, fulfill obligations fight, & finish to keep you faith

We realize all is so trivial & long for what is good & infinite.

11. Elijah did not hesitate to cross the Jordan (2 Kings 2:8). Paul keenly anticipated his future when he would wear a "crown of righteousness" (2 Timothy 4:8). How does your daily obedience or disobedience affect your anticipation of being with God eternally?

Days of obedience long for God, & days of disobedience we long for more time to change.

12. As Christians, we affirm that Christ Jesus was "taken up" (Acts 1:9), and as God's children, we inherit his Spirit (Ephesians 1:13-14) just as Elisha inherited Elijah's mantle. How does confidence in the resurrection and ascension of Christ help us live a life of obedience to God?

TRUTH.

Share

Fence Co,
— wisdom
— laborers

Baby

Drew

School

Me

Elijah in the
New Testament

MARK 1:2-8; LUKE 1:13-17; 9:28-36

Certain types of people show up on every page of history. Take, for instance, the political dictators like Julius Caesar, Napoleon, and Hitler. The brilliant artists and musicians —Michelangelo, Beethoven, and Picasso. The dedicated teachers such as Socrates or Anne Sullivan. And don't forget the pairs of loyal friends—Jonathan and David, Lewis and Clark, Ruth and Naomi, Churchill and Montgomery.

We rarely hear, however, of an actual *person* showing up more than once in the course of world history. And yet Elijah's story does not end with his whirlwind trip to heaven. The prophet appears in the New Testament in two ways. First, he passes through figuratively as the backdrop for the ministry of John the Baptist. Then he comes literally with Moses as a visitor on the mountaintop during the transfiguration of Jesus.

In this great event we get a final glimpse of Elijah, who was still alive when Jesus came to earth—just as he is today. God allowed his great prophet to have direct dealings with his Son.

And this reward for obedience brings our study to a worthwhile close.

Last Question

1. If, after you died, God were to send you back to earth to do something special for him, what would you want your mission to be?

We would know firsthand of heaven's extravagance + God's goodness (but we already do). We would tell others but why wait!!

READ MARK 1:2-8 AND LUKE 1:13-17.

2. In what ways did John the Baptist demonstrate the "spirit and power of Elijah"? From what you know about Elijah and John the Baptist, how were the two prophets similar?

Both preached on punishment for sin.
Both argued king + queen of their time
Both assoc c desert.
Luke 1:16

3. How were the ministries of both Elijah and John works of restoration? Why did the Lord need a forerunner to prepare the people for his coming?

Elijah's time very few godly people.
John's no prophets for several hundred years.
Needed to prepare them.

4. How are people made ready and prepared for the Lord? What do you think it means for the hearts of fathers to be turned toward their children?

Hearts must be changed, minds must be refocused

READ LUKE 9:28-36.

5. What may have been the subject of Elijah's and Moses' conversation with Jesus? Why would these two men have been chosen to meet with God's Son at this point in his life?

Great prophets of the Old Testament meet The Prophet!

v 33?

6. What significance might this experience have had for Peter, James, and John?

Reaffirmed Christ's claims prior to His death & resurrection.

7. It is crucial to note that, before the Transfiguration, Jesus warned his disciples about how he was going to die (Luke 9:22-27). Glory is usually preceded by suffering. How was this true in Elijah's life? How has it been true in your life?

Persecuted & ran his whole life.
Being a Christian is never easy.

✗ 8. Discuss the relationship between obedience, suffering, and reward. How can you put this truth into practice in your life as both Jesus and Elijah did in theirs?

Me – obediance → suffering but unsure in what way as of yet.

Elijah – obediance to truth led to persecution by King/Queen – etc.

Jesus – obvious his obediance to truth led to others jealousy & his death.

9. Think back on your study of Elijah and consider his three mountaintop experiences: Mount Carmel (study 4), Mount Horeb (study 6), and the Mount

of Transfiguration. What did Elijah's experiences in each place teach him about faith? obedience? God's plan?

Carmel - Showdown c̄ Baal worship. Saw God's awesome power.

Horeb - Hiding from Jezebel Saw God's all seeing self. Cannot hide

Transfiguration - c̄ Moses & Christ Saw Christ in bodily form

10. Share how Elijah's life encourages you to be obedient in a threatening world. In what specific ways has your encounter with this prophet of God helped you grow in faith and obedience?

Boldness. Following Christ is not easy. We live in a fallen world & difficulties & negativity & pursuit of worldly matters abound

Shane

Labovers

Fencing co.
House hunting

Drew

Jennie's B-day
HCV
School   Patience ē colleagues

Andy

D.J.
Work going well
Good time ē Carol
Conversation ē Mom
Indian couple

Leader's Notes

Study 1: Obedience in Spite of the Times

Before beginning this study, have your group read the Historical Review on page 3.

Note on 1 Kings 16:29–17:7. After Jericho's famous destruction, the city was never rebuilt. See Joshua 6:26-27 for the prophecy concerning the consequences detailed in 1 Kings 16:34.

Question 5. Elijah's appearance in the Hebrew Scriptures comes abruptly. Unlike the accounts of Moses and Samuel, no childhood stories are told that foreshadow the significance of this prophet. All we know for certain is that, although he was a Tishbite (from Tishbe, a small settlement in eastern Galilee), Elijah lived in an area east of the Jordan known as Gilead, a rugged pastoral area of Israel. (See map on page x.)

Question 6. See Deuteronomy 11:16-17. Drought was a judgment promised by God for the sin of idolatry.

Question 9. God told Elijah to go, so he had to wait until God told him to leave.

Question 12. Help the group expand its thinking by considering not only modern-day Ahabs but global and national influences that are in opposition to God. Encourage them to look at these kinds of influences in their own lives.

Question 13. See James 5:17-18.

Study 2: Obedience in Spite of Circumstances

Question 2. Read 1 Kings 16:31. Zarephath was located in Sidon, which was under the control of Queen Jezebel's father.

Question 8. When answering this question, discuss the circumstances of need as well as abundance, deprivation as well as provision. Discuss how both of these extremes can hinder us from obeying God.

Question 9. To help assess the widow's feelings, consider what she was expecting in 1 Kings 17:12.

Study 3: Obedience in Spite of Danger

Question 3. We often tell ourselves that God would never ask us to do something too irrational or too dangerous. Perhaps we get this impression from Paul's statement that God "will not let you be tempted beyond what you can bear" (1 Corinthians 10:13). There's a great difference, however, between being *tempted* and being *challenged*. God challenged many people in Scripture—such as Abraham, Elijah, and Mary—with incomprehensible tests. But he was always there to help them, just as he is here for us today.

Question 4. Although Obadiah called Elijah his master, Elijah corrected him and directed him back to Ahab. We see from Obadiah's fear and unwillingness to do what Elijah commanded that his allegiance really was to Ahab. Perhaps you can discuss how our true loyalty sometimes shows up through our fears precisely as Obadiah's did.

Question 9. Discuss how when we abandon the Lord's commands and the moral law he has set for us, we will typically obey other voices that lead us into the immorality that Satan demands.

Study 4: Obedience in Spite of Impossibilities

Question 6. Be specific, taking care that the discussion is profitable for the group in terms of spiritual growth rather than being an occasion for griping.

Question 9. Just as a parable is a concrete illustration of a specific concept, the altar was a concrete example of the state of the nation, which was once whole but had become broken and useless. The twelve stones represented the twelve tribes of Israel and reminded the people who they really were. Elijah's efforts to rebuild Israel so that she could once again bring glory to God, and the Lord's desire to heal his people, came to the forefront in the act of repairing the altar.

Question 10. Try to identify areas of unanswered prayer that may be hindered by a lack of personal surrender.

Question 11. Refer to 1 Kings 18:36-37. The central problem with Israel's idolatry is that they've forgotten who they are. By addressing God as the God of Abraham, Isaac, and Jacob, Elijah reminds the people of who they are and to whom they belong. Elijah's actions in 1 Kings 18:31 also serve to remind the people of their historic identity. Discuss ways in which we forget who we are and to whom we belong, as well as ways that the Lord reminds us of our identity when we go astray.

Question 13. Keep in mind that in order to have a pure church body, each person in that body must get rid of the impurities in his or her own life.

STUDY 5: OBEDIENCE IN SPITE OF DELAY

Question 4. The NIV translation of the Bible doesn't *say* he was praying, but it can be safely inferred.

Question 7. We can surmise a couple of reasons why Elijah needed to get to Jezreel before Ahab. Since Ahab seemed to be afraid of both Jezebel and Elijah, he probably wouldn't have wanted to admit to his wife that he had been beaten. So perhaps Elijah wanted to arrive first to make sure that Jezebel heard the true story of what had happened to all her priests on Mount Carmel. Or maybe, in God's mercy, Elijah wanted to give Ahab a last chance to turn away from Baal and back to God before Jezebel's influence dissuaded him.

Question 8. Share with the group the strengths and weaknesses you identified, then discuss possible reasons for the weaknesses and difficulties the group expressed.

Question 10. Persistent prayer is an act of obedience: It centers on faith in what God says, not merely on the evidence of circumstances.

Question 11. One simple way to pray for the needs expressed is to have each person pray for the individual next to him or her.

Study 6: Obedience in Spite of Discouragement

Question 3. See the map in front of the book for the location of Beersheba in Judah. See 1 Kings 17:2,8 and 18:1,46 for hints on what important detail was missing.

Question 4. Consider physical, spiritual, emotional, mental, and social circumstances. How often our weariness and loneliness provide an easy slide away not only from trust but from reason!

Question 5. The "angel of the Lord" in Hebrew Scriptures is a heavenly being sent by God as his representative to deal directly with humans. The "angel of the Lord" functions both as an agent of destruction and judgment (2 Samuel 24:16; 2 Kings 19:35) and of protection, deliverance, guidance, and instruction (2 Kings 1:3; Daniel 3:28). "In many passages he [the angel] is virtually identified with God as an extension of the divine personality" (J. D. Douglas, ed., *The New Bible Dictionary,* Wheaton, Ill.: Tyndale House Publishers, 1982, p. 38).

Question 7. Mount Horeb, also known as Mount Sinai, was a holy place for the Jews. There God met with Moses and gave him the Ten Commandments and the plans for his people's place of worship, the tent-tabernacle.

Question 11. One beneficial way to get out of depression is to focus on others. Apparently, this was just the remedy God planned for Elijah. After anointing his successor, Elijah began setting up "discipleship schools" to train others in God's ways. This visionary work for God kept him from self-centered brooding.

STUDY 7: OBEDIENCE IN SPITE OF MARTYRDOM

Question 1. Since most of us haven't seen literal martyrdom, try to discuss the term in a broader sense. Persecution or unjustified punishment happen often in our society.

Note on 1 Kings 21. Dating from the sequence of kings in Judah and Israel, approximately six years have passed since Elijah returned to continue God's work in his turbulent native country. During these years, Ahab and his wicked queen continued to resist the rule of Jehovah in their hearts and in Israel. Twice God defeated Syria and brought victory to Ahab in spite of Israel's greatly inferior army (1 Kings 20). Still Ahab was disobedient. Contrary to God's explicit instruction, he spared the life of Ben-Hadad, the king of Syria. A young prophet rebuked Ahab for his disobedience and foretold the subsequent downfall of his house and ultimately of Israel. This study begins as Ahab, without a hint of repentance, returned home "sullen and angry" (1 Kings 20:43).

Question 2. See Leviticus 25:23 and Numbers 36:7 for biblical reasons why Naboth would not give up his land.

Question 5. See Matthew 10:39 and John 12:25-26.

Question 7. Second Kings 9:25-26 reveals that Jehu—who would eventually overthrow Ahab's son and see to the bloody extermination of Ahab's family—and Bidkar, Jehu's officer, were riding with Ahab in his newly acquired vineyard. While admiring the king's ill-gotten spoil, they heard the prophecy of Elijah declaring the end of Ahab's dynasty.

Question 9. See Luke 12:15-21 for further discussion.

Question 10. The fulfillment of the prophecy concerning Ahab is recorded in 1 Kings 22:34-38, and that concerning Jezebel in 2 Kings 9:30-37.

STUDY 8: OBEDIENCE IN SPITE OF OFFENSE

Question 2. Ahaziah may have broken his neck when he fell through the lattice in his upper chamber. Baal-Zebub, literally the "fly-god," was worshiped as a ruler of evil spirits. In Mark 3:22, the teachers of the Law accuse Jesus of casting out demons through *Beelzebub,* the prince of demons. These two names may be referring to the same spirit.

Question 4. Take note of this description; it will come up again in study 10.

Question 9. Remember that Ahaziah's mother, Jezebel, was still alive and well!

Question 11. Like Elijah, Jesus also confronted those who hated him. He cared enough about them to confront them in love and in hope that they would repent. It would have been much easier for him, and for Elijah, to ignore and cut off those who offended him.

Study 9: Obedience in Spite of Death

Question 2. The company of the prophets was a gathering of men around a key teacher or rabbi, much like Jesus and his disciples. Paul, too, encouraged this type of schooling: "The things you have heard me say in the presence of many witnesses entrust to reliable men who will also be qualified to teach others" (2 Timothy 2:2). "If the church were to consistently follow this advice, it would expand geometrically as well-taught believers would teach others and commission them, in turn, to teach still others. Disciples need to be equipped to pass on their faith" (*Life Application Bible,* Wheaton, Ill.: Tyndale House Publishers, 1988, p. 2200).

Question 5. In the Hebrew tradition, the eldest son inherited a double portion of his father's possessions. Elisha's request to Elijah came from the heart of a son who wanted to carry on his father's work and fulfill the obligation of the eldest son.

Question 6. After offering to do whatever Elisha asked, it may seem strange that Elijah left it up to God to decide whether to grant the younger prophet's request. But Elijah was testing Elisha to see how he would respond when given the option to stay behind and to ask for whatever he wanted. And Elisha passed with flying colors.

Elijah knew that only one step remained for Elisha to truly inherit the double portion of his spirit: "To see the transactions of the spirit-world requires a spirit of no ordinary purity, and of no ordinary faith. No mere mortal eye could have beheld that fiery cortege. To senses dulled with passion, or blinded by materialism, the space occupied by the flaming seraphim would have seemed devoid of any special interest.… Perhaps there was not another individual in all Israel with heart pure enough, or spiritual nature keen enough, to have been sensible of that glorious visitation" (F. B. Meyer, *Elijah and the Secret of His Power*, Hants, United Kingdom: Marshall Pickering, 1986, pp. 143-44).

Question 9. Elisha's words in verse 14 were not spoken out of irreverence for God; rather, they were a desperate request that God be with him.

Question 12. "It becomes us…to walk as Elijah did, with alert and watchful spirit; talking only on themes that would not be inconsistent with an instantaneous flash into the presence of God. Thus, whenever our Father's carriage comes for us; and wherever it overtakes us…may we be prepared to step in, and 'sweep through the gates, washed in the blood of the Lamb'!" (Meyer, *Elijah and the Secret of His Power*, pp. 143-44).

STUDY 10: ELIJAH IN THE NEW TESTAMENT

Question 2. See Malachi 4:5-6 for Old Testament prophecies concerning Elijah and John the Baptist. See also Matthew 17:10-13 and John 1:19-34. Remember when Ahaziah's servants described Elijah as "a man with a garment of hair and with a leather belt around his waist" (2 Kings 1:8)? How well Mark's description of John the Baptist matches! Other similarities include:

- Both Elijah and John made enemies of the
  king—and even more, the queen—of their
  respective regions by speaking out against sin.
- They both were associated with the desert.
- They both preached hell, fire, and brimstone,
  and called the people of Israel to repentance.

Question 3. "Important Roman officials of this day were always
preceded by an announcer or herald. When the herald arrived
in town, the people knew that someone of prominence would
soon arrive" (*Life Application Bible,* p. 1725).

Question 4. The Living Bible translation of Luke 1:17 reads:
"He will soften adult hearts to become like little children's."
John brought the people to repentance, helping them recognize their sin and soften their hearts toward God. Like children, they became more pliable in God's hands. Wasn't Elijah's
ministry similar—helping the people recognize their idolatry
and leading them toward repentance?

Question 5. Moses was a chief representative of the Law, and
Elijah was a chief representative of the prophets. Since Jesus
was the fulfillment of both the Law and the prophets, it's fit-
ting that these two ambassadors would meet with him right
before his death, which satisfied the Law's requirement of a sacrifice for sin and fulfilled the prophets' predictions of a Savior.

Question 8. According to Romans 8:5-11, we are always obeying *something*—either sin or righteousness. If we obey sin, we
will suffer the consequences; if we obey righteousness—in
spite of godly suffering—God will reward us.

What Should We Study Next?

To help your group answer that question, we've listed the Fisherman studyguides by category so you can choose your next study.

TOPICAL STUDIES

Angels by Vinita Hampton Wright

Becoming Women of Purpose by Ruth Haley Barton

Building Your House on the Lord: Marriage and Parenthood by Steve and Dee Brestin

The Creative Heart of God: Living with Imagination by Ruth Goring

Discipleship: The Growing Christian's Lifestyle by James and Martha Reapsome

Doing Justice, Showing Mercy: Christian Actions in Today's World by Vinita Hampton Wright

Encouraging Others: Biblical Models for Caring by Lin Johnson

The End Times: Discovering What the Bible Says by E. Michael Rusten

Examining the Claims of Jesus by Dee Brestin

Friendship: Portraits in God's Family Album by Steve and Dee Brestin

The Fruit of the Spirit: Growing in Christian Character by Stuart Briscoe

Great Doctrines of the Bible by Stephen Board

Great Passages of the Bible by Carol Plueddemann

Great Prayers of the Bible by Carol Plueddemann

Growing Through Life's Challenges by James and Martha Reapsome

Guidance & God's Will by Tom and Joan Stark

Heart Renewal: Finding Spiritual Refreshment by Ruth Goring

Higher Ground: Steps Toward Christian Maturity by Steve and Dee Brestin

Images of Redemption: God's Unfolding Plan Through the Bible by Ruth Van Reken

Integrity: Character from the Inside Out by Ted Engstrom and Robert Larson

Lifestyle Priorities by John White

Marriage: Learning from Couples in Scripture by R. Paul and Gail Stevens

Miracles by Robbie Castleman

One Body, One Spirit: Building Relationships in the Church by Dale and Sandy Larsen

The Parables of Jesus by Gladys Hunt

Parenting with Purpose and Grace by Alice Fryling

Prayer: Discovering What the Bible Says by Timothy Jones and Jill Zook-Jones

The Prophets: God's Truth Tellers by Vinita Hampton Wright

Proverbs and Parables: God's Wisdom for Living by Dee Brestin

Satisfying Work: Christian Living from Nine to Five by R. Paul Stevens and Gerry Schoberg

Senior Saints: Growing Older in God's Family by James and Martha Reapsome

The Sermon on the Mount: The God Who Understands Me
by Gladys Hunt

Spiritual Gifts by Karen Dockrey

Spiritual Hunger: Filling Your Deepest Longings by Jim and
Carol Plueddemann

A Spiritual Legacy: Faith for the Next Generation by Chuck
and Winnie Christensen

Spiritual Warfare by A. Scott Moreau

The Ten Commandments: God's Rules for Living by Stuart
Briscoe

Ultimate Hope for Changing Times by Dale and Sandy
Larsen

Who Is God? by David P. Seemuth

Who Is Jesus? In His Own Words by Ruth Van Reken

Who Is the Holy Spirit? by Barbara Knuckles and Ruth Van
Reken

Wisdom for Today's Woman: Insights from Esther by Poppy
Smith

Witnesses to All the World: God's Heart for the Nations
by Jim and Carol Plueddemann

Women at Midlife: Embracing the Challenges by Jeanie
Miley

Worship: Discovering What Scripture Says by Larry Sibley

BIBLE BOOK STUDIES

Genesis: Walking with God by Margaret Fromer and
Sharrel Keyes

Exodus: God Our Deliverer by Dale and Sandy Larsen

Ezra and Nehemiah: A Time to Rebuild by James Reapsome

(For Esther, see Topical Studies, *Wisdom for Today's Woman*)

Job: Trusting Through Trials by Ron Klug

Psalms: A Guide to Prayer and Praise by Ron Klug

Proverbs: Wisdom That Works by Vinita Hampton Wright

Ecclesiastes: A Time for Everything by Stephen Board

Jeremiah: The Man and His Message by James Reapsome

Jonah, Habakkuk, and Malachi: Living Responsibly
    by Margaret Fromer and Sharrel Keyes

Matthew: People of the Kingdom by Larry Sibley

Mark: God in Action by Chuck and Winnie Christensen

Luke: Following Jesus by Sharrel Keyes

John: The Living Word by Whitney Kuniholm

Acts 1–12: God Moves in the Early Church by Chuck and
    Winnie Christensen

Acts 13–28, see *Paul* under Character Studies

Romans: The Christian Story by James Reapsome

1 Corinthians: Problems and Solutions in a Growing Church
    by Charles and Ann Hummel

Strengthened to Serve: 2 Corinthians by Jim and Carol
    Plueddemann

Galatians, Titus, and Philemon: Freedom in Christ
    by Whitney Kuniholm

Ephesians: Living in God's Household by Robert Baylis

Philippians: God's Guide to Joy by Ron Klug

Colossians: Focus on Christ by Luci Shaw

Letters to the Thessalonians by Margaret Fromer and Sharrel
    Keyes

Letters to Timothy: Discipleship in Action by Margaret
    Fromer and Sharrel Keyes

Hebrews: Foundations for Faith by Gladys Hunt

James: Faith in Action by Chuck and Winnie Christensen

1 and 2 Peter, Jude: Called for a Purpose by Steve and Dee
  Brestin
How Should a Christian Live? 1, 2, and 3 John by Dee
  Brestin
Revelation: The Lamb Who Is a Lion by Gladys Hunt

BIBLE CHARACTER STUDIES

Abraham: Model of Faith by James Reapsome
David: Man After God's Own Heart by Robbie Castleman
Elijah: Obedience in a Threatening World by Robbie
  Castleman
Great People of the Bible by Carol Plueddemann
King David: Trusting God for a Lifetime by Robbie
  Castleman
Men Like Us: Ordinary Men, Extraordinary God by Paul
  Heidebrecht and Ted Scheuermann
Moses: Encountering God by Greg Asimakoupoulos
Paul: Thirteenth Apostle (Acts 13–28) by Chuck and
  Winnie Christensen
Women Like Us: Wisdom for Today's Issues by Ruth Haley
  Barton
Women Who Achieved for God by Winnie Christensen
Women Who Believed God by Winnie Christensen